THE HUMAN BODY IN 3D

THE MOUTH AND NOSE IN 3D

rosen publishing's
rosen
central

ISOBEL TOWNE AND
JENNIFER VIEGAS

Published in 2016 by The Rosen Publishing Group, Inc.
29 East 21st Street, New York, NY 10010

First Edition

Library of Congress Cataloging-in-Publication Data

Towne, Isobel.
The mouth and nose in 3D/Isobel Towne and Jennifer Viegas.
    pages cm.—(The human body in 3D)
Includes bibliographical references and index.
Audience: Grade 5 to 8
ISBN 978-1-4994-3609-9 (library bound) — ISBN 978-1-4994-3611-2 (pbk.) —
ISBN 978-1-4994-3612-9 (6-pack)
1. Mouth—Juvenile literature. 2. Nose—Juvenile literature. 3. Taste—Juvenile literature. 4. Smell—Juvenile literature. I. Viegas, Jennifer. II. Title.
QM306.T69 2016
611'.31—dc23
                                           2015000139

Manufactured in the United States of America

CONTENTS

INTRODUCTION

We talk, laugh, eat, and smell every day, and most of the time we probably don't give it that much thought. Meanwhile, our mouths and noses are hard at work together with other organs to bring us all these sensations. There's a whole lot going on in our 8.8-pound- (about 3.9-kilogram-) skulls!

For example, when someone goes to bite into a chocolate chip cookie, a lot of parts are at work. The jaw is made up of mandible (lower jaw) and maxilla (upper jaw). Muscles of the face and neck help the lower jaw, which is the only one of the two jaw parts that moves, along. These muscles are so strong that the jaw can chomp down on that cookie with a force of 200 pounds (close to 91 kilograms)!

Meanwhile, inside the mouth are many important parts, such as the tongue, which has a lot of responsibilities of its own. It helps the teeth with chewing, moves to help make different sounds, and tastes. Humans are born with 10,000 taste buds on their tongues, but that number decreases as they age. Made up almost entirely of muscle, the muscles at the back of the tongue also help with swallowing. Many people have heard that the tongue is the strongest muscle in the body. It's not. In fact, the tongue is made up of 8 separate muscles. (Although it depends

When you pick up a mug of cocoa, you smell the fragrance of chocolate. The sense of smell is more powerful than the sense of taste.

on one's definition of "strongest," the main muscle in your jaw, known as the masseter, is often considered a nominee.)

At the back of the mouth is the throat, which points food and air in the right directions. Air from the nose is ushered into the trachea, or windpipe, to be moved along to the lungs. Food and drink to the esophagus and onward to the stomach.

There's plenty to know about the nose, too. It's divided into two narrow parts called the nasal fossae, which are divided by the septum. Mucus, which makes many queasy, actually cleans dust and other unwanted things from the air inhaled. Mucus carries these substances out of the body. Meanwhile, the sinuses offer backup, making more mucus when it's needed. Sinuses have a number of other duties, such as offering support to the face for those unfortunate falls or punches.

The sense of smell is actually a lot stronger than the sense of taste. When one gets a whiff of garlic, the knowing nose's cilia send messages to the brain, which instantly identifies this pungent odor. The area of the brain associated with this activity is known as the olfactory area, and it is close to the area that controls emotions, mood, and memory. This is why when one smells something delicious, like apple pie baking or garlic sautéing on the stove, his or her mouth begins to water as they picture the food in question.

Not everything about these body parts we use all the time are easy to explain. Consider the mysterious uvula, for example: Scientists are still puzzling over what it does! Read on to learn more about what experts think it's used for. This resource holds a whole lot more information about the nose and mouth.

CHAPTER ONE

BITE, CHEW, AND SWALLOW

Most people have seen human head skeletons. Museums often display replicas, and models are a popular Halloween holiday decoration, too. These models usually are lightweight, but real human heads on average weigh 8.8 pounds (about 3.9 kilograms). That is like carrying a bowling ball on your shoulders all day and night. Thankfully, strong bones and muscles in the neck hold up the head.

The skeleton part of the head, called the skull, functions like a box made of bones. It holds and protects all of the important organs located in the head. These include the brain, ears, eyes, nose, and mouth.

Although the skull looks like one big bone, it actually consists of twenty-nine separate bones. The section of bone encasing the brain is called the cranium, which is made up of eight connected bones. Fourteen interlocking bones frame the nose, mouth, and eyes. The hole where the nose is located reveals how air can enter the body.

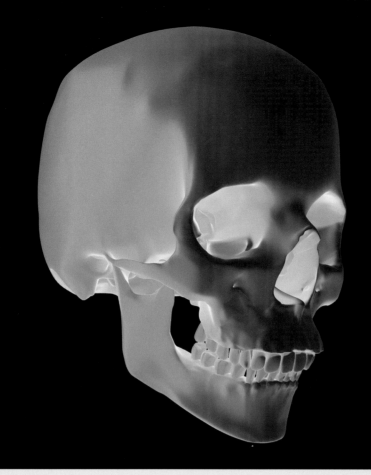

It's fun to scare visitors with skull Halloween decorations, but real human head skeletons are much heavier. Most weigh almost 9 pounds (4.1 kilograms).

MAXILLA AND MANDIBLE

The jaw has an upper and lower section. The upper jaw, called the maxilla, consists of two bones. The lower jaw, referred to as the mandible, is hinged where it meets the upper jaw. This enables the mandible to move up and down, while the top part of the jaw stays relatively still. To get an idea of how this works, stretch out all the fingers of one hand, except the thumb. Next, move the thumb up and down. Here the fingers work like the maxilla and the thumb serves as the mandible.

Muscles stretching from the neck to the top of the head help to close the lower jaw. These muscles are incredibly strong. They allow the jaw to close with a force of 200 pounds (almost 91 kilograms)! Such strength gives the jaw the power to crush hard foods like nuts and raw vegetables. It is even

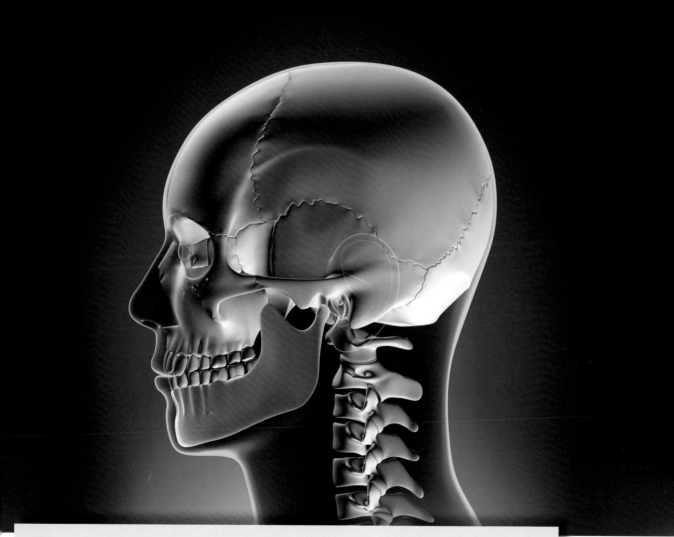

The jaw is made up of two sections: the lower jaw, or mandible, is hinged to the maxilla, or upper jaw, so it can move up and down. The maxilla is made up of two bones.

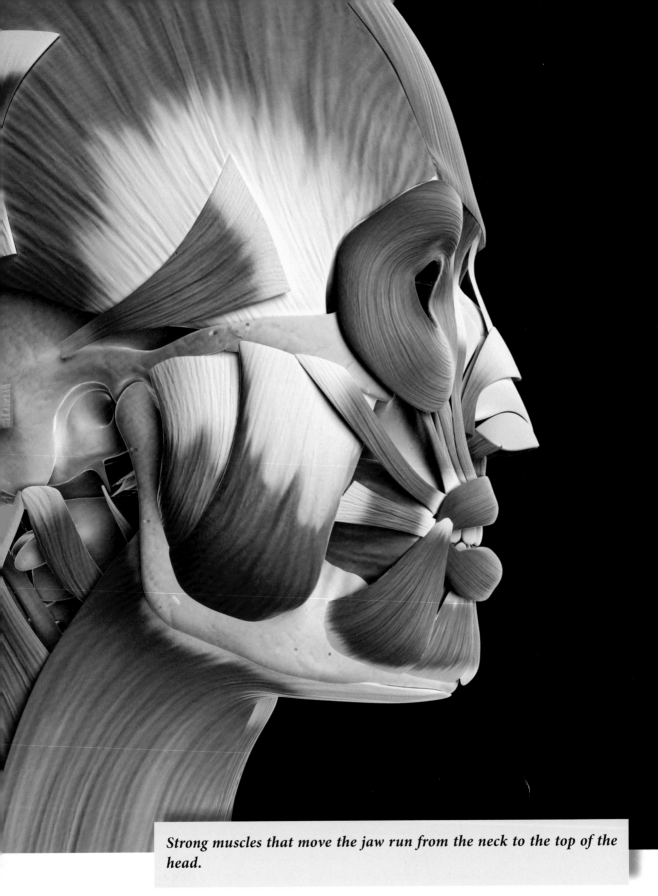

Strong muscles that move the jaw run from the neck to the top of the head.

possible to feel the strong muscles controlling the jaw. To do this, clench the teeth together tightly. Next, hold a hand near the lower jaw and then near the temple above the eyes. What are felt are just a few of the muscles that give the jaw its impressive strength.

The jaw, along with the skeleton, grows from birth until an individual is about 20 years old. A newborn infant has a very small jaw. That is one reason why babies have such soft features and must consume special baby food, which is often pureed or finely chopped. By the time the person is 6 years old, the lower jaw has greatly increased in size. At 20, both the upper and lower jaws have fully developed.

ANOTHER REASON TO SMILE

The extraordinarily flexible mouth is one of the face's most expressive features. Holding the lips tightly together can show concern or anger. An open mouth indicates surprise. A down-turned mouth suggests sadness, while an upturned, open mouth causes the whole face to lift up into a smile.

Frowning actually requires a lot more energy and effort than smiling. Forty-three muscles are activated with a frown, but only seventeen are required to produce a smile. Smiling, therefore, promotes relaxation and helps to prevent certain wrinkles. It is the world's best facelift!

WHAT'S IN THE MOUTH

Set in between the upper and lower jaw is the mouth, with the lips forming an entrance to the mouth's interior. Glancing in a mirror reveals that the lips do not look like they are covered with the same kind of skin that surrounds the rest of the body. This is because the lips are made from a unique set of muscle fibers and elastic tissue. The fibers and tissue that form the lips are like a cross between regular skin and the membrane, or thin covering, lining the inside of the mouth. Unlike most skin, the lips have no hairs or sweat and oil glands. Glands are organs that secrete, or leak out, certain substances like hormones and saliva.

Taking a look inside the mouth, the top is bound by a part of the upper jaw known as the hard palate. It is hard because the tongue and lower jaw need something to push up against to crush food. Resting alongside the hard palate is the soft palate, which extends back into the throat. This tissue, more tender than the hard palate, moves upward when food is swallowed. Without the soft palate, food would shoot up and out of the nose!

A u-shaped piece of tissue hangs in the back center of the mouth from the soft palate. This tissue is called the uvula. Often cartoons show characters yelling with their mouths wide open, revealing the uvula. Its function in the mouth and throat remains a mystery, as scientists still are unsure what it does. Many believe it helps to close off air passages coming from the nose, lessening the chances of choking on food.

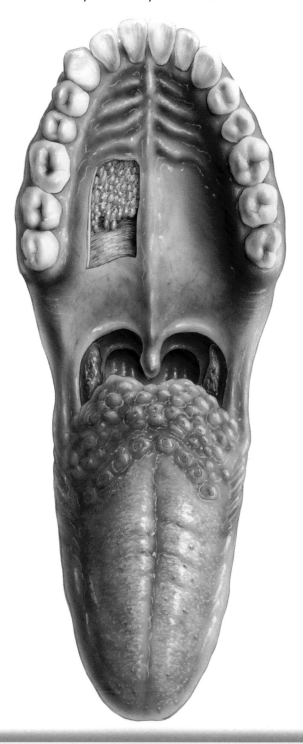

The hard and soft palates, on the roof of the mouth, work with the tongue to crush and move food. The tongue is covered with vallate papillae, which contain taste buds.

Underneath the hard and soft palates are the tonsils. These two organs help to remove germs that may enter the throat from food and air. Sometimes the tonsils become infected—most often in children—and must be removed.

DOWN THE THROAT

Leading from the back of the mouth and down into the neck is the throat. It is the area that directs air from the nose to the lungs, and food and liquids from the mouth into the stomach. The throat is divided into two main parts: the pharynx and the larynx.

The pharynx is a muscular passage that extends from the nose to the esophagus, the tube-like structure that sends food to the stomach. About 5 inches long, the pharynx is the crossroads for movement of air, food, and liquids. Not everything goes down to the stomach, however. Like trains switching tracks, air can be redirected down through the trachea into the lungs.

The trachea, or windpipe, looks a bit like a vacuum cleaner hose. Just as a hose has plastic for flexibility and support, the trachea has rings of cartilage surrounding it. The cartilage rings prevent the trachea from collapsing and allow for intake of different levels of air. Tiny hair-like appendages called cilia stick out of a slimy membrane lining the trachea. They help to keep the throat clean and ensure that food and water move smoothly.

The trachea has a flap of cartilage above it called the epiglottis. Like a lid, the epiglottis closes the entrance to the windpipe when

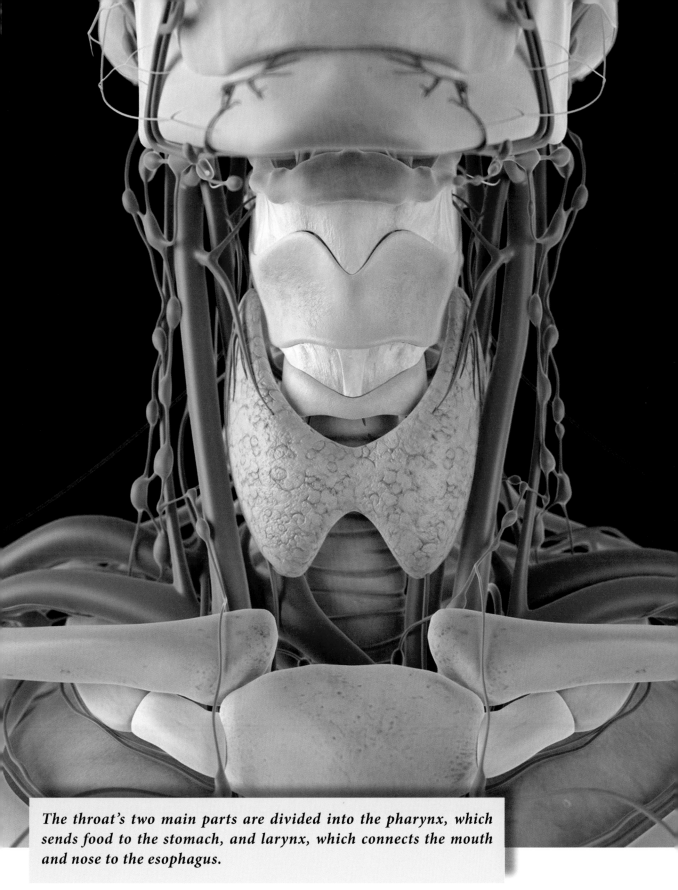

The throat's two main parts are divided into the pharynx, which sends food to the stomach, and larynx, which connects the mouth and nose to the esophagus.

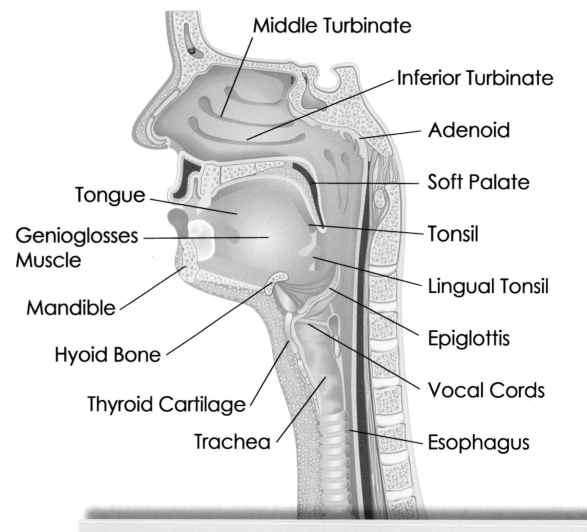

The anatomy of the throat. Your throat moves air from the nose to the lungs and directs food and liquid in your mouth to your stomach.

food is swallowed. Without it, food and liquid could wind up in the lungs instead of the stomach.

Above the trachea are the thyroid glands, which together look like a bowtie in the throat. The thyroid glands control fuel use in the body, calcium levels, and growth. They are protected

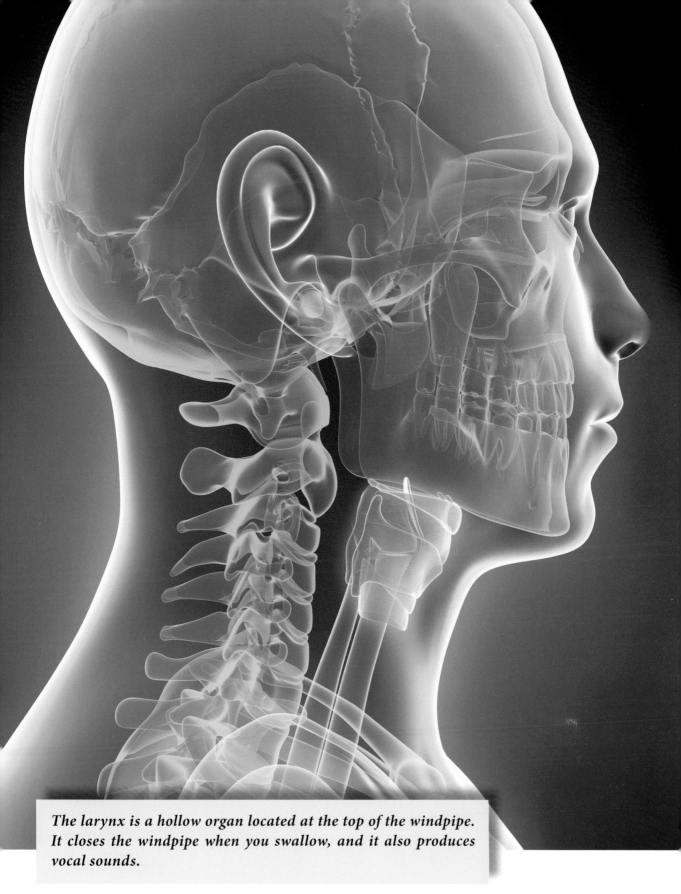

The larynx is a hollow organ located at the top of the windpipe. It closes the windpipe when you swallow, and it also produces vocal sounds.

by a section of cartilage commonly called the Adam's apple, which is the largest of nine cartilages in the larynx, or voice box. This cartilage sticks out like a bump in the throat. The bump is particularly noticeable in men, as they generally have larger larynxes than women.

INTO THE LARYNX

Before air travels from the nose to the trachea it must first move across the larynx, a triangular box about 1.6 inches (4.06 cm) long that opens behind the tongue in the throat. The inside looks like a tube with a slit in the middle lined on both sides with white reedy material. This material forms the vocal cords.

When breathing, the vocal cords open to allow air to flow freely down the trachea. When speaking, the cords draw closer together. Airflow makes the cords vibrate, which produces sound waves. The tightness of the cords determines the rate of vibration and pitch. Larynx size also affects the sound. People with small voice boxes generally have high-pitched voices while large larynxes produce lower tones. That is why men tend to have deeper voices than women.

CHAPTER TWO

TIME TO EAT

Food powers the human body, similar to the way gasoline fuels a car. Humans eat food to provide their bodies with the energy that drives almost all activities, from basic functions like the heart beating to high-energy movements such as swimming. The more active a person is, the more energy, or food, he or she requires.

Of course, the human body is much more sophisticated than a car. Food not only gives energy, but it also provides nutrients that promote the body's ability to grow and maintain itself. These nutrients include proteins, carbohydrates, fats, oils, minerals, and vitamins. Different foods contain varying amounts of these nutrients, which is why it is important to eat a balanced diet. Nuts, for example, are high in protein, while vegetables are high in fiber, minerals, and vitamins.

Food cannot enter the stomach as is. Imagine swallowing a whole banana. It must first be chewed into a manageable pulp.

In addition to the jaw muscles, muscles all around the face, including those in the lips and cheeks, control chewing. The lip and cheek muscles primarily hold the food in place so that the teeth can do their job.

BITE INTO IT: THE TEETH

Teeth may seem like hard, lifeless objects, but they are very much alive. These bone-like structures are attached to the jaws as though they were plants growing out of soil. Teeth have two main jobs. First, they bite into food and chop it into pieces that can be managed in the mouth. Second, teeth crush, munch, and pulverize food into a mashed-up pulp that can be swallowed.

The period of tooth loss as a child marks the development of permanent teeth. Before that time, individuals have what are known as milk teeth. Milk teeth cells begin to form in the womb, even

At six months, babies start to grow a set of twenty milk teeth, also known as primary, temporary, or deciduous teeth. As a child gets older, a set of permanent teeth grows in.

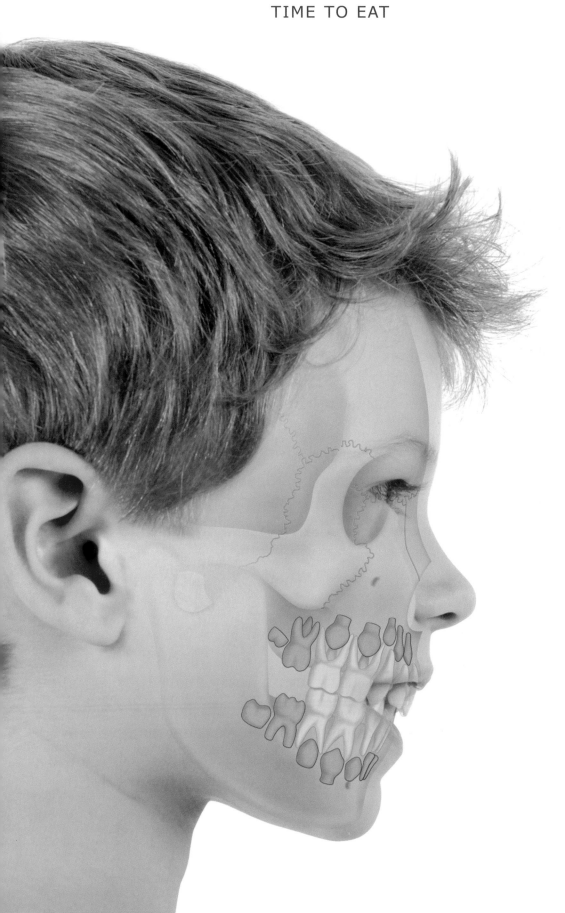

before a baby is born. At birth, young infants possess thick gum pads, which contain the cells necessary for teeth development. When the baby reaches about 6 months of age, teeth begin to erupt. Their emergence continues until about the age of 2, when the child usually has a full set of 20 milk teeth. After the age of six, the milk teeth begin to fall out and are replaced by permanent teeth. By the age of 20, most people should have a set of 32 teeth, if wisdom teeth and other teeth are not removed or accidentally knocked out.

Permanent teeth can be divided into four types: incisors, canines (also called eyeteeth), premolars, and molars. Incise means to cut and that is just what incisors do. These teeth have a narrow edge shaped like a knife blade. Incisors cut or bite into food and chop it into small pieces. To see what they look like, smile in a mirror and look at the front teeth. These are incisors.

Canine teeth are located to the sides of the incisors. They rip and tear food apart. Think of biting into a chewy piece of bread or meat. The mouth opens wider to expose the canines so they can tear off bite-sized morsels. While incisors have a flat edge on the bottom, canines are pointed. This can be felt by running the tongue over them.

Premolars are like a cross between a canine and a molar. They have slightly more jagged edges than canines. The main job of premolars is to cut and chew. Usually this action is done to pieces of food bitten off by the incisors and canines.

Molars have a wide exposed surface area that enables them to chew and crush. Given their shape and location at the back of the gum line, molars are not effective at cutting and biting.

TIME TO EAT

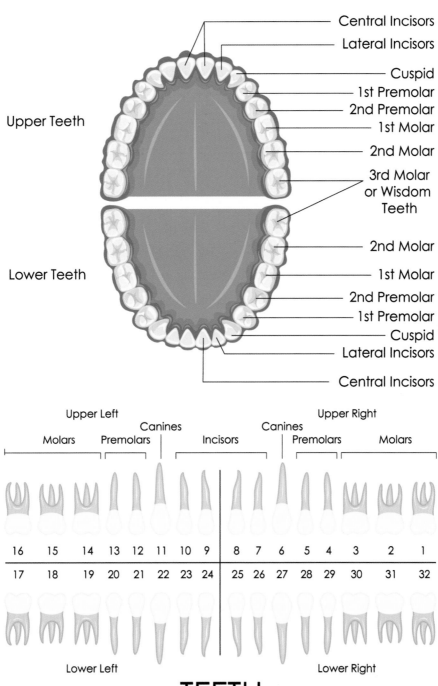

Central Incisors
Lateral Incisors
Cuspid
1st Premolar
2nd Premolar
1st Molar
2nd Molar
3rd Molar or Wisdom Teeth

Upper Teeth

2nd Molar
1st Molar
2nd Premolar
1st Premolar
Cuspid
Lateral Incisors
Central Incisors

Lower Teeth

Upper Left — Molars — Premolars — Canines — Incisors — Canines — Premolars — Molars — Upper Right

16 15 14 13 12 11 10 9 | 8 7 6 5 4 3 2 1
17 18 19 20 21 22 23 24 | 25 26 27 28 29 30 31 32

Lower Left   Lower Right

TEETH

An adult has a total of thirty-two permanent, also called secondary or adult, teeth. They are made up of incisors, canines, premolars, and molars.

They grind food that has already been cut up by the other teeth. Wisdom teeth are molars that erupt in 75 percent of people by the time they reach the age of 18. A throwback to earlier stages in human evolutionary development, wisdom teeth often do not fit properly in the jaw, which has gotten smaller among all people over time. In such cases, the wisdom teeth must be extracted. A museum with skeleton models of early human ancestors is a great place to see how big their jaws and mouths were.

FROM CROWN TO ROOT

On the outsides, teeth come in almost as many shapes and sizes as people. On the inside, however, they essentially are the same. Each tooth consists of two main parts: the crown and the root. The crown is the portion of the tooth that is visible in the mouth. The root is the part that is embedded within the jaw. When a tooth falls out or is extracted, the root can be seen as a pointy, hard tip on the bottom of the tooth.

Each tooth is made up of several layers: Enamel on the outside, dentin next, and at the center is the pulp cavity. Cementum connects the tooth to the jawbone.

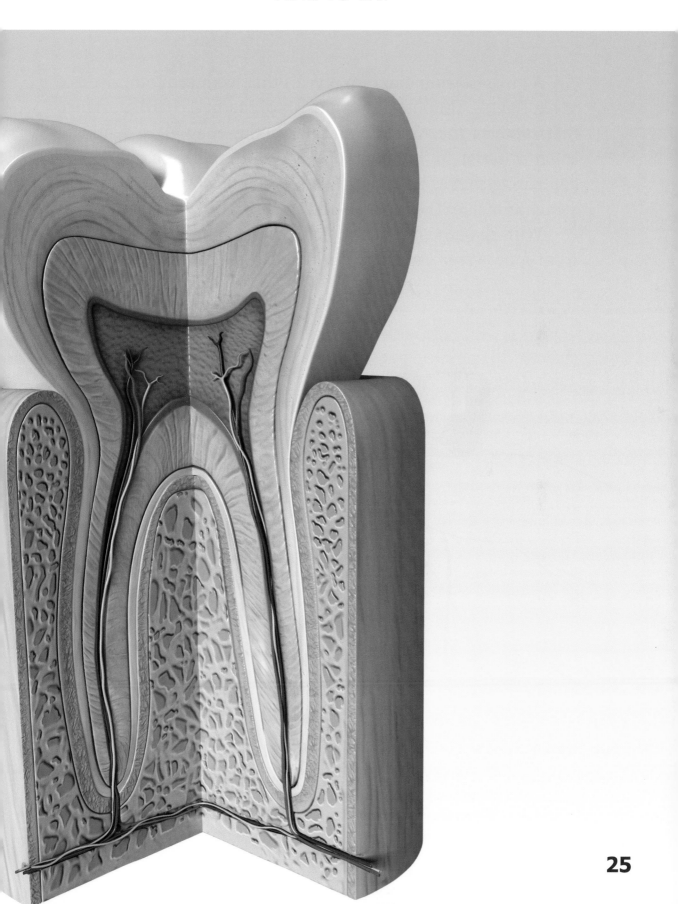

A cross-section diagram reveals that teeth are comprised of several layers. The outer layer consists of enamel, a hard substance that protects the tooth. Underneath the enamel is dentin, a softer material. In the center of every tooth there is a pulp cavity containing nerves and blood vessels. Finally, a material called cementum glues the tooth in place within the jawbone.

With all of their nooks and crannies, teeth can hold bacteria from food. Over time this may lead to plaque, a combination

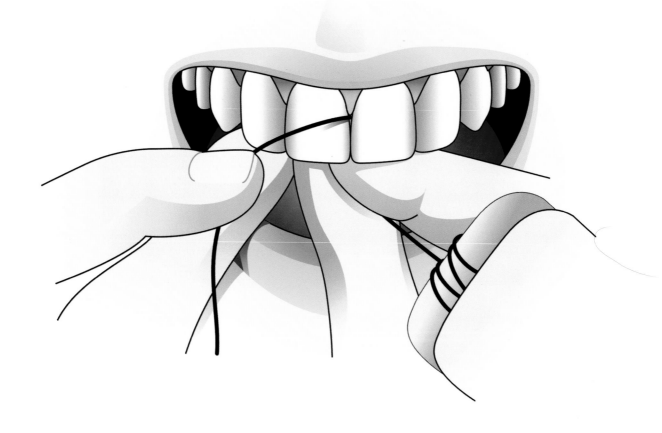

Brushing your teeth is a great first step for a clean healthy mouth, but proper flossing can reach the tiny, tight spaces a toothbrush may miss.

of rotting food, bacteria, and other tooth-decaying substances. If the bacteria are not removed by brushing, they can produce acids that may eat through the enamel and into the dentin. The resulting damage creates a cavity. Dentists fill cavities because the infection could spread to the pulp, then into the jawbone, where it could lead to blood poisoning. It is, therefore, very important to brush the teeth after every meal and to visit a dentist regularly.

ALL ABOUT FLOSS

Toothbrushes often miss the tight areas between teeth, so it is also important to floss daily. Waxed and unwaxed dental flosses are available. Both work well when used properly.

To floss, wind an 18-inch piece of floss around the middle fingers of each hand. Using the thumbs and forefingers, slide the floss between each tooth, gently scraping any plaque off the tooth sides. Repeat with a clean section of floss for each area in the mouth. After flossing, rinse the mouth thoroughly with water or mouthwash.

THE LONG JOURNEY OF FOOD

When a drink or a snack enters the mouth, it begins a journey that can extend more than 20 feet. That is because the mouth is the entryway for the digestive system of the body. Food is first chewed into a ball called a bolus. The tongue pushes the

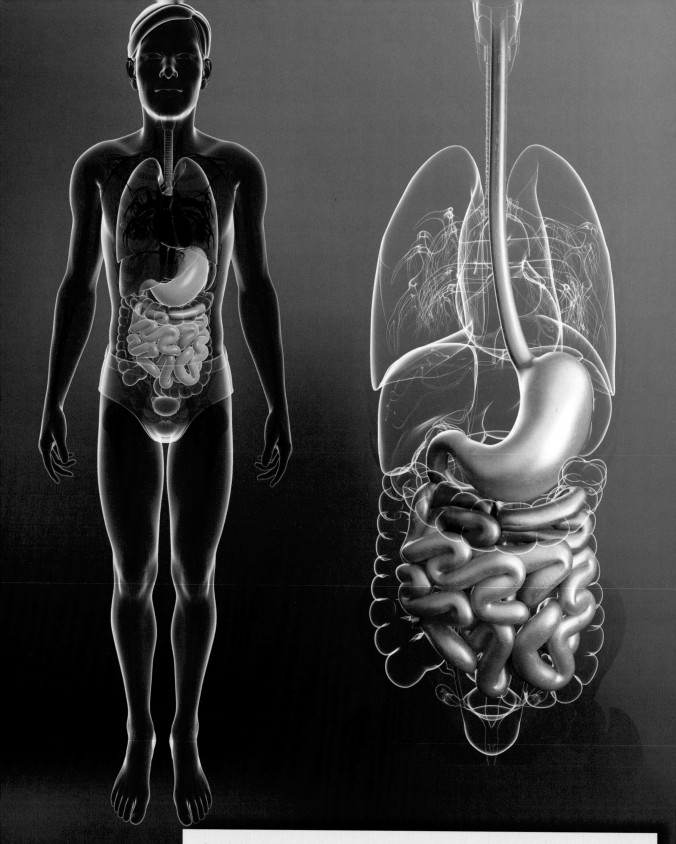

That bite of pizza is tasty, but chewing is just the beginning of a 20-foot (6.1 m) trip through the digestive system, including the small intestine.

bolus toward the back of the pharynx. When the ball of food touches the throat a series of chain reactions occur that induce swallowing.

As the throat muscles push food downward, the soft palate moves upward to prevent the bolus from going up the nose. The epiglottis then seals the trachea closed. Sometimes the lid-like epiglottis does not close fast enough, often when a person is eating and talking at the same time, which can cause a choking feeling because food or liquid has entered the lungs.

Usually, however, the epiglottis does its job correctly, and food is sent down the esophagus. Try placing the fingers of one hand on either side of the top of the throat while swallowing.

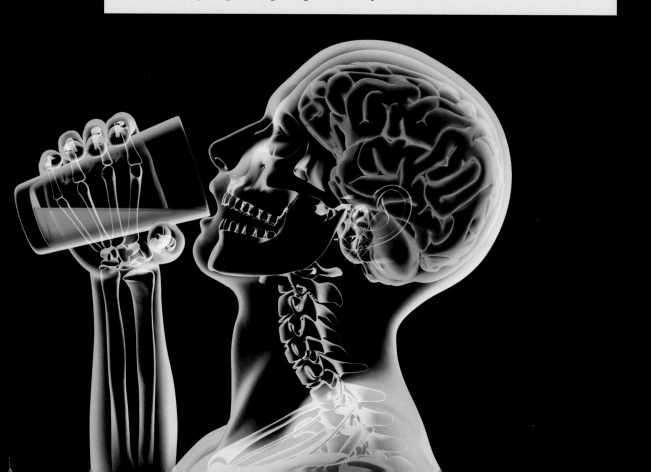

Drinking and eating begin the digestive process at the mouth, but swallowing is more than just pouring a liquid down your throat.

Notice how swallowing is not as simple as pouring water down a drain, but instead requires several movements. Muscle contractions, known as peristalsis, push the food in waves to the stomach. Thanks to peristalsis, a person could eat sitting sideways or upside down and the food would still get to the stomach.

The stomach showers its contents with digestive juices that break the food down into a liquefied pulp. The pulp then travels through the small and large intestines. Part of the small intestine, called the jejunum, allows the nutrients in the food to pass into blood, which carries the nutrients throughout the entire body.

CHAPTER THREE

GETTING TO KNOW THE NOSE

Few people realize that their bodies are home to what could very well be the world's best air conditioners. And, as the saying goes, it's as "plain as the nose on your face." The nose takes in air and expels gaseous waste, and it

The nose that's so plainly on your face is anything but simple. Its complicated structure lets you breathe—in addition to filtering air—and identify smells.

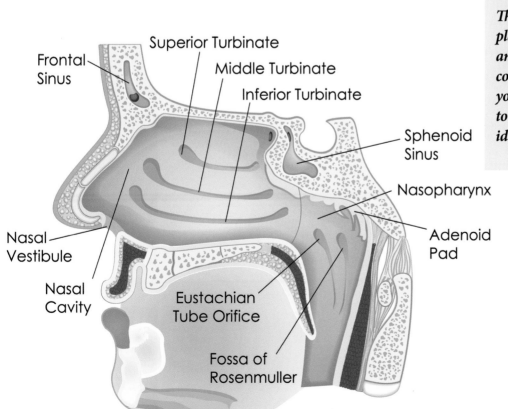

Frontal Sinus

Superior Turbinate

Middle Turbinate

Inferior Turbinate

Sphenoid Sinus

Nasopharynx

Nasal Vestibule

Adenoid Pad

Nasal Cavity

Eustachian Tube Orifice

Fossa of Rosenmuller

also filters out irritants, such as dust and dirt. The nose then warms and moistens air so that it can circulate properly to the lungs and then to the rest of the body. Mechanical air conditioners require constant external maintenance and repair, but the nose is a self-sufficient powerhouse that continues to work throughout a healthy person's lifetime.

The exterior part of the nose gains its shape and structure from bone and cartilage. Cartilage gives the nose a certain amount of flexibility, while bones attach the nose to the skull. One area of attachment can be felt by placing the thumb and forefinger at the bridge of the nose near the eyes.

Inside, the nose is divided into two narrow sections called the nasal fossae. The divider is called the septum. Like the outside of the nose, the septum is made from bone and cartilage. It is covered with a delicate lining referred to as the mucus membrane. This membrane helps to keep the nose warm and moist. Lining the nostrils are several tiny strong hairs. These hairs protect the entrance of the nose and help to filter out large particles.

The interior of the nose is divided into two thin cavities, called nasal fossae, which are separated by the wall of cartilage known as the nasal septum.

3D
Ex: 7519
Se: 102
Volume

DFOV 1
STND/+

R

8

1

No VOI
kv 120
mA 420
Rot 0.50
1.2mm
Tilt: 0.0
08:35:50
W = 409

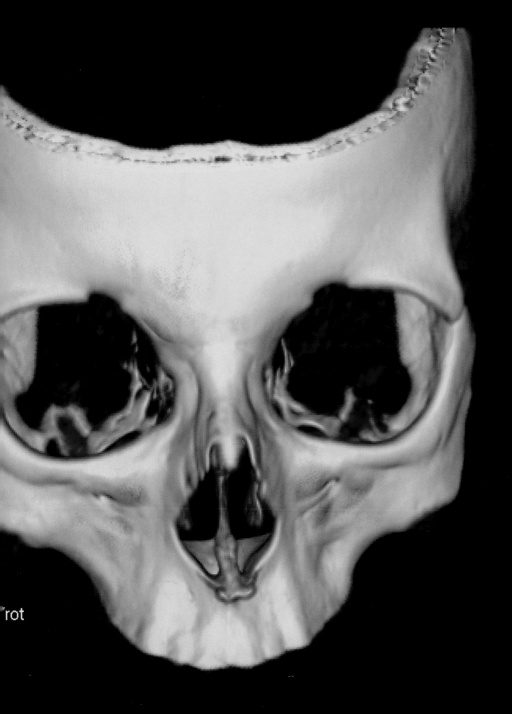

SP

k cut

rot

Centre Cardiologique du Nord

****

F 36 287982

Feb 08 2006

L

8

5

IA

UP THE NOSE

Behind the fossae is a bone divided into three parts by ridges. Together the ridges are called the nasal conchae. They look like three slides because they rise near the brain region and then slope downward before dividing into the fossae.

Between each concha—the singular for conchae—is a passage called the meatus (pronounced mee-aye-tuss). As with the septum, the meatus is lined with a mucous membrane, except this membrane has a very rich blood supply. As a result, and because of its structure, the meatus is active in warming and moistening air that is breathed in from the nose. Mucus helps in this process.

Most people think of mucus as a disgusting substance that only occurs with a cold. Actually the meatuses in an average person secrete nearly a pint of mucus each day. Look at a pint of milk in the grocery store to get an idea of how much is made. This

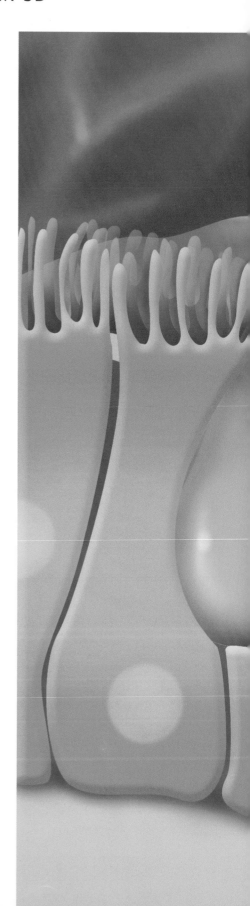

Mucus collects waste, which is moved and drained out of the nose by the cilia. When you have sinusitis, the mucus cannot drain and causes congestion and infection.

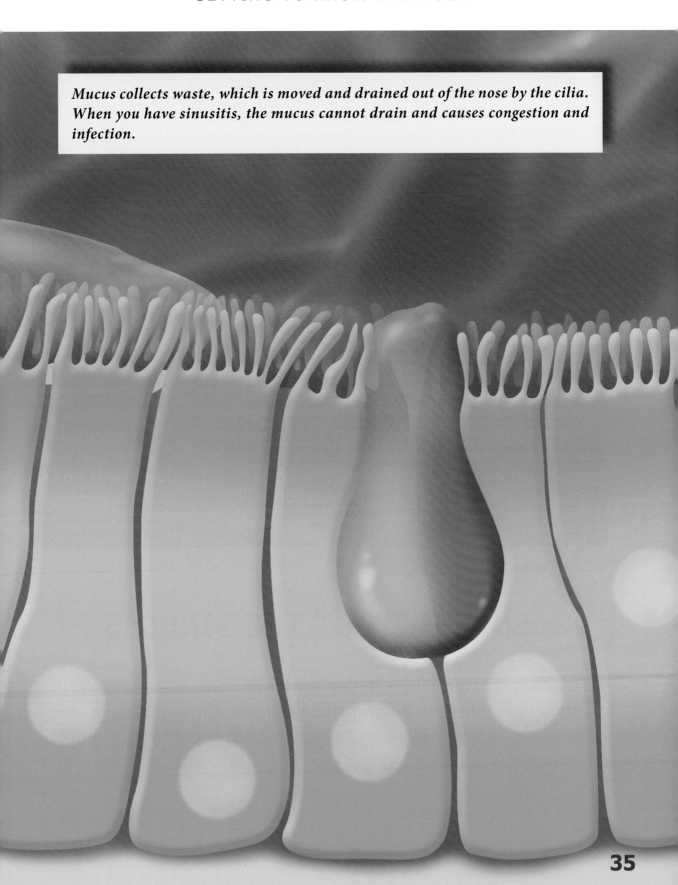

slimy substance is like an air cleaning fluid. It flows over cilia on the meatuses and enables them to trap dust and other undesirable things in air. The cilia move the waste material, collected in mucus, out of the nose region and into the throat where they can be swallowed and then disposed of by the body.

SCRUTINIZING THE SNEEZE

Sneezes help to rid the lungs and nose of irritants, such as pollen, dust, or germs. One or more of these irritants may settle on the mucus membrane in the nose. When this happens nerves immediately send a signal to the breathing muscles, which begin a sneeze.

First, the individual takes a sudden deep breath, causing the lungs to expand. The airways then burst open, the eyes close, and the lungs shoot out their contents through the mouth and nose, likely forcing the irritant out of the body.

SNIFFING OUT THE SINUSES

Sinuses are eight holes in the head. They are located between the eyes and nose, behind the eyebrows, and in back of the cheeks. They produce mucus when the nose does not make enough. They also help to give the face some resistance to

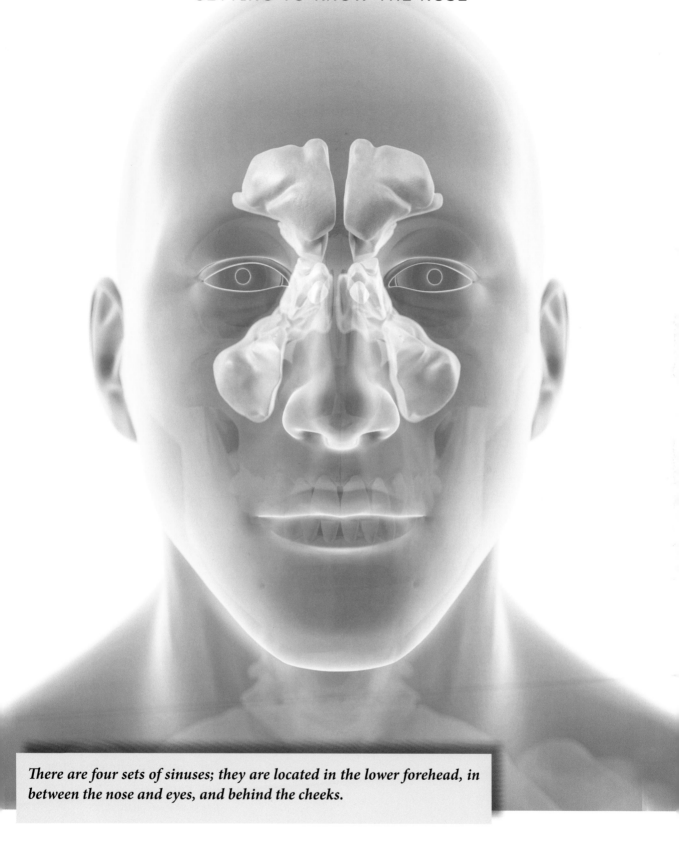

There are four sets of sinuses; they are located in the lower forehead, in between the nose and eyes, and behind the cheeks.

impacts, such as punches to the head or falls on hard surfaces. The sinuses decrease the weight of nasal bones. They also give resonance, or an appealing vibration and tone, to the voice. Individuals with a beautiful singing voice often owe much of their natural talent to the shape and structure of their sinuses, along with the flexibility of the vocal cords.

WHAT'S THE CONNECTION?

Because the nose and ears both lead to the throat, the activities of the nose can affect the ears. Blowing the nose too hard can rupture the eardrum. It may also send germs in nose mucus into the sinuses near the ears, which could cause an ear infection.

The mouth also has a connection to the ears via the throat. For example, chewing gum often relieves pressure on the ears when flying in an airplane

The ears, nose, and mouth are all intricately connected, so what happens to one part affects the others. For example, chewing bubble gum can help relieve pressure in your ears.

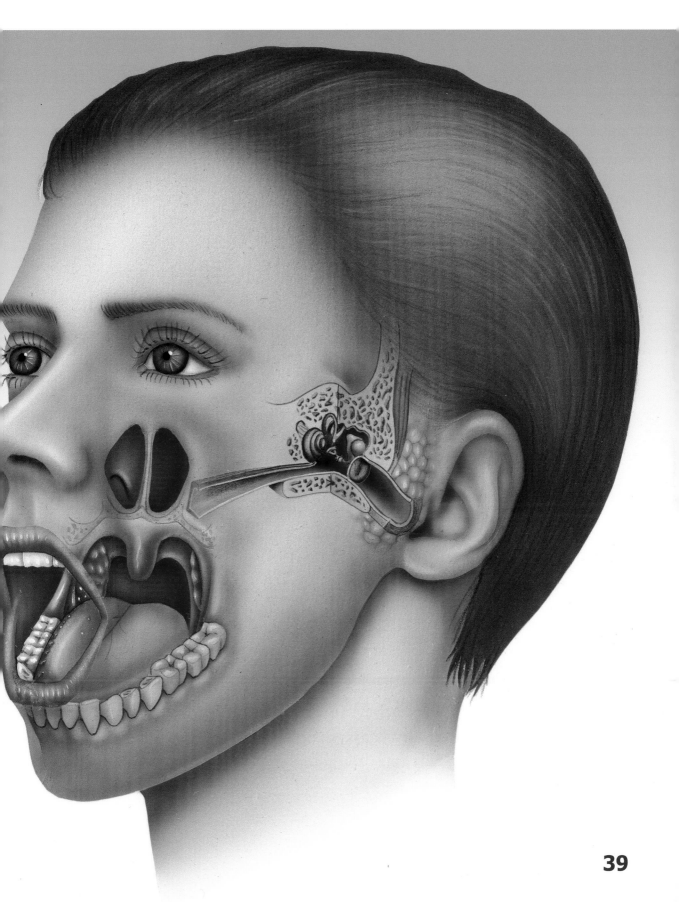

or making a sudden descent in an underground subway. That is because the chewing sensation may cause the connection between the ear and the throat—the Eustachian tube—to open and release air. Normally, the Eustachian tube can do this on its own, but sometimes quick changes in pressure cause it to retain air and create a popping sensation in the ears.

INHALE AND EXHALE

At rest, most people breathe about 12 times a minute. During strenuous exercise the breathing rate can go up to 80 times per minute. In fact, every day each individual breathes in and out 5,000 gallons of air. People also breathe while sleeping, of course. Snoring, by the way, can occur when a person breathes through the mouth while sleeping, which is often because of a partial blockage of the nose and throat. The uvula at the back of the mouth vibrates, causing the snoring sound.

Breathing is part of a process known as respiration. The purpose of respiration is to supply the body with oxygen, which helps to release energy and to burn food. Oxygen is essential to human life. While people can go without food for a day or so, it would be impossible to exist without oxygen.

Respiration also involves the release of carbon dioxide, which is a waste product of certain processes within the body. Oxygen is breathed in and carbon dioxide is exhaled. Respiration normally is an involuntary activity, meaning that

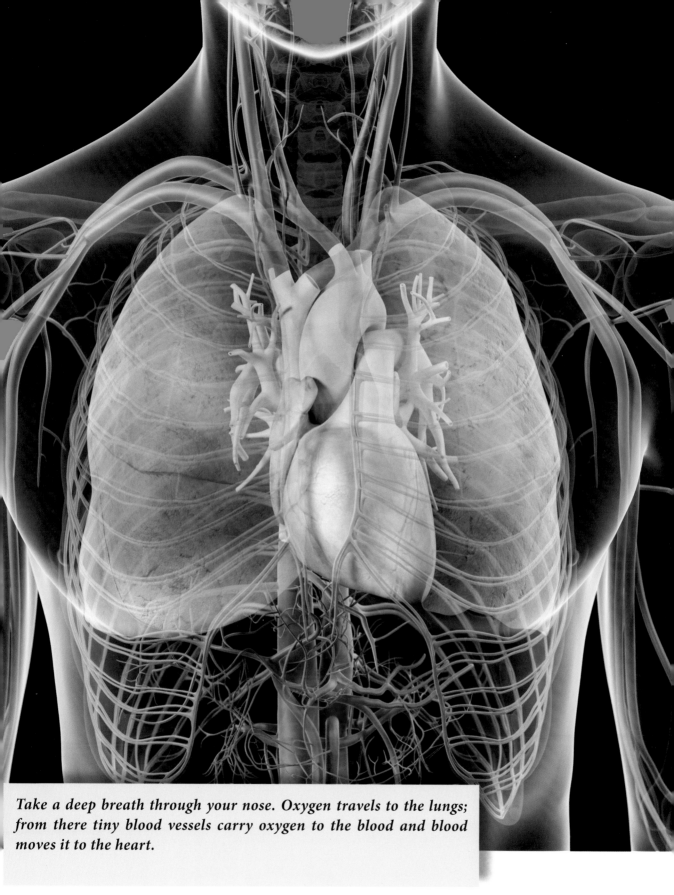

Take a deep breath through your nose. Oxygen travels to the lungs; from there tiny blood vessels carry oxygen to the blood and blood moves it to the heart.

people do not have to consciously think about breathing for it to happen. However, it is possible to control breathing. For example, think of taking a deep breath before swimming or blowing up a balloon.

The oxygen inhaled from the nose travels down the trachea and into the lungs. A muscle below the lungs called the diaphragm performs most of this work. It can be felt going up and down with each breath. Capillaries, or tiny blood vessels surround the lungs. They transport the oxygen to blood. Like a car that has just been filled with gasoline, the oxygenated blood then is transported to the heart, which pumps the energized blood throughout the body. Exhaling is the opposite of inhaling. The blood transports carbon dioxide to the lungs. The lungs send the carbon dioxide up through the trachea and throat where it can be released through the nose or mouth.

Although it is possible to breath through the mouth, it is much better to do so through the nose, because the nose can filter out unwanted dust and germs. There are times, however, when a huge gust of air is desired. That is one reason why people sometimes breathe through the mouth after strenuous activity.

Breathing can become difficult when the inside of the nose and the sinuses become inflamed, or swollen with mucus. Germs are not the only culprits. Many people are allergic to certain pollens and molds. When inhaled, these cause allergy victims to produce protective agents called histamines that increase mucus production and help to rid the body of the airborne irritant. That is why people with allergies tend to wheeze and sneeze a lot. Antihistamine drugs provide some relief, but the best prevention is to avoid breathing the irritant in the first place by staying indoors.

CHAPTER FOUR

TASTING AND SMELLING

Five senses—smell, taste, sight, touch, and hearing—connect humans to the world around them. Smelling and tasting are controlled by the mouth and nose. The sense of taste is the least developed of all five senses, meaning that it provides less information about the external world than sight, smell, touch, and hearing. Still, taste does help to identify food and makes life a lot more fun.

TAKING A LOOK AT THE TONGUE

Stick out your tongue in front of a mirror. Based on what is visible, the tongue looks sort of like a shoe sole. There is, however, more to the tongue than meets the eye. The tongue actually fills most of the lower part of the mouth above the mandible. It also extends into the front of the throat because it is attached to the epiglottis. People may pride themselves on their arm or leg muscles, but

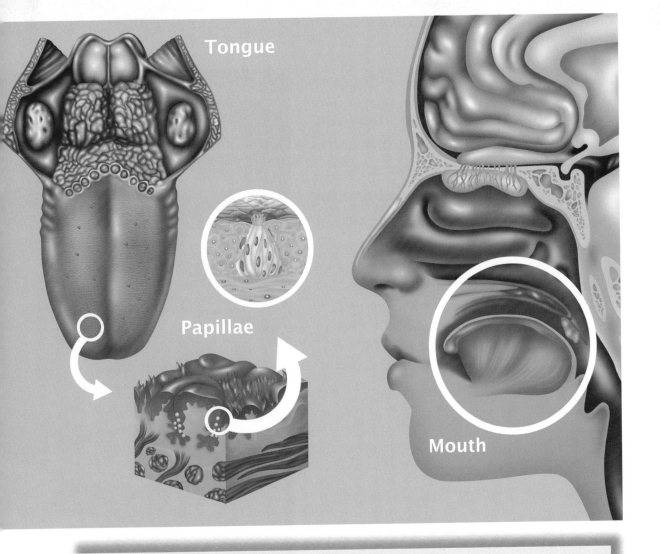

Tongue

Papillae

Mouth

The top of the tongue (left) is covered with papillae (bottom inset), which contain the taste buds (top inset). Taste buds help identify what you are eating.

the tongue is one of the most active and mobile muscles in the body. It can move up and down, from side to side, in circles, and can even curl up on itself.

Teeth are rooted in the lower jaw, and so is the tongue. It is attached by two muscles—the geniohyoid and mylohyoid—and a bone called the hyoid. The hyoid bone, which sort of looks like a boomerang, is fixed just below the epiglottis flap. The job of the mouth muscles, including the tongue itself, is to move and process food. Taste buds on the surface of the tongue inform the individual about what he or she is eating or drinking.

TAKE A TASTE: TASTE BUDS

It is a misconception that the visible bumps on the tongue are individual taste buds. These tiny projections are called papillae. Between each papilla are tiny spaces or ridges. The spaces form mini moats around the papillae. Food and liquid roll off the papillae and seep down into the ridges, where many taste buds are located. Taste buds also are present on the palates and on the inside of the throat.

Taste buds are made out of tiny receptor cells. Each cell has a small hair-like projection

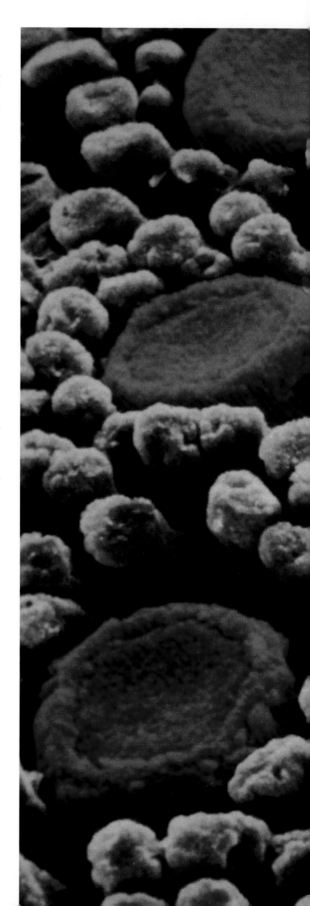

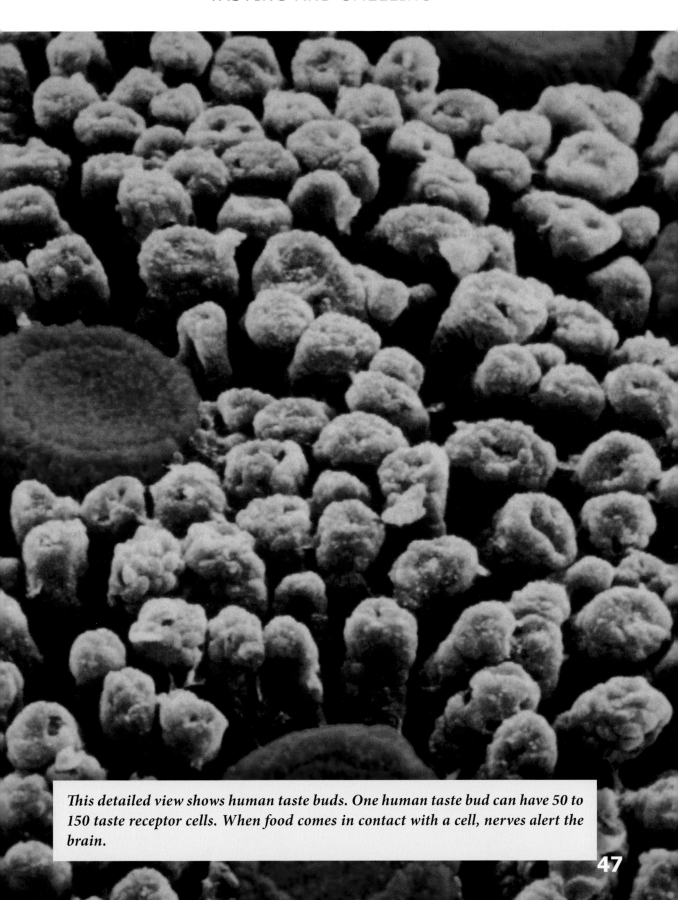

This detailed view shows human taste buds. One human taste bud can have 50 to 150 taste receptor cells. When food comes in contact with a cell, nerves alert the brain.

sticking out of it. These projections are called microvilli. Food coming into contact with the receptor cells sends a message to the brain through a network of nerve fibers. Because each person has about 9,000 to 10,000 taste buds, this process could get confusing, but all the impulses channel into two main nerve bundles.

It is amazing to think that taste buds only respond to four basic tastes: sweet, salty, sour, and bitter. Think of how many different foods are consumed and how unique each tastes. The distinctive flavor of each food comes from varying combinations of the four basic tastes, along with the food's texture, smell, and other qualities.

While researchers still are analyzing how the taste buds pick up individual flavors, it generally is thought that buds at the tip of the tongue respond to sweet tastes. The sides of the tongue, just behind the tip, are believed to detect salty flavors. Sour tastes are picked up behind the salty detectors. Bitter flavors are identified toward the back center of the tongue. It is interesting that the tongue is 8,000 times more sensitive to bitter tastes than it is to sweet ones. That is why bitter medicine often is flavored with a sweetener. The sweetness makes the medicine more palatable, or pleasing to the taste buds on the tongue and palate.

Some foods do not get their flavor from the taste buds. Hot chilies or other spicy foods gain most of their punch by stimulating nerves on the tongue that are sensitive to pain. It can be a pleasant sensation, though, particularly for people who are used to the stimulating jolt.

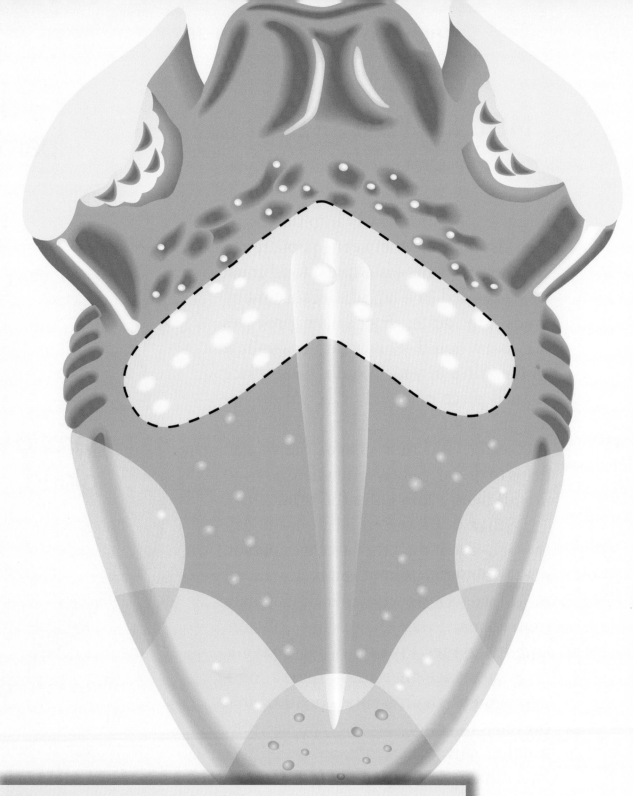

The tongue detects four main tastes in four general areas: sweet (at the tip, shown here in purple), salt (in blue), sour (yellow), and bitter (green).

MOUTH-WATERING: SALIVA

du
paroti

Because food must travel into the moat-like depressions between papillae to reach most of the taste buds, food must be suspended in a liquid. Because many foods are quite dry, saliva provides necessary liquid. For example, swallow all the saliva in your mouth. Next, place a small piece of bread or cereal on the tongue. Hold it there for a few seconds and see if it has much flavor. Saliva also helps to digest, or break down, foods and liquids before they enter the stomach.

parotid
gland

Saliva is produced 24 hours a day. In fact, each day the average person makes about 3 pints (about 1.4 liters) of saliva. Saliva contains four main ingredients: water, mucus, ptyalin, and lysozyme. Ptyalin is an enzyme, or a substance that helps digest food. Lysozyme is an antiseptic chemical that prevents infections from forming in the mouth. Saliva, therefore, acts a bit like an antibacterial soap in the mouth.

The saliva that helps break down a bite of pizza is created thanks to the cooperation of three sets of glands: parotids, sublingual, and submandibular, which are connected by ducts.

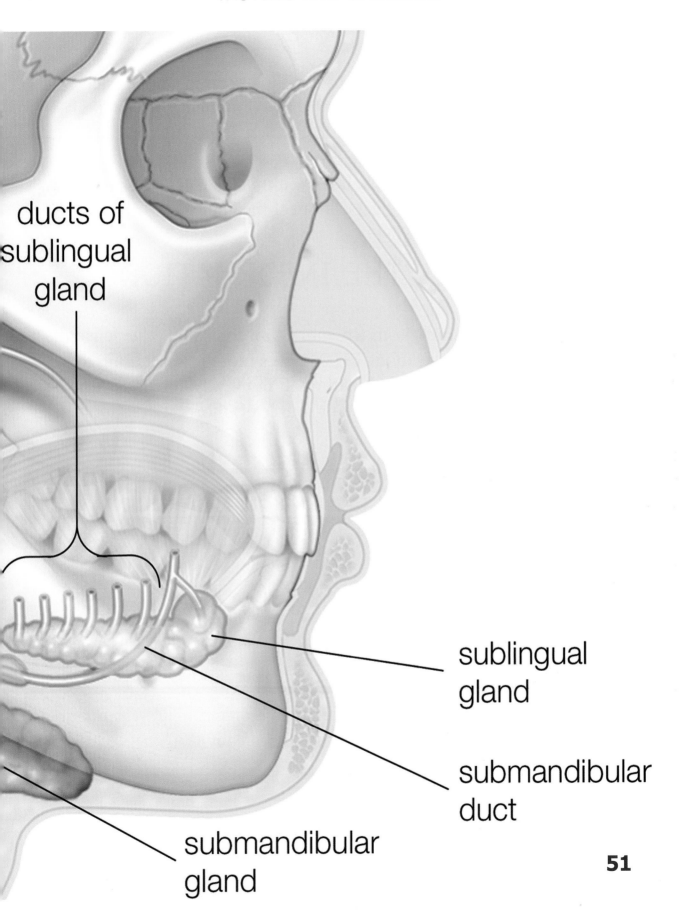

ducts of
sublingual
gland

sublingual
gland

submandibular
duct

submandibular
gland

Three pairs of glands produce and secrete saliva. Each set creates a different mixture that, when combined together, makes saliva. For example, the parotids, which are located in the neck near the jaw and ear, create a watery solution with lots of ptyalin. The sublingual glands, however, make a thick, mucus-filled saliva. Small tubes, or ducts, connect the glands.

SMELL THE INFORMATION

The sense of smell is much more powerful than the sense of taste. It would take about 25,000 times more of something to be tasted instead of smelled. Although not always obvious, smelling provides us with a constant source of information about the

ANIMALS AND INSECTS: THEIR NOSES KNOW

Pet owners know that if a treat snack is hidden someplace out of the way, the pet usually can sniff around and find it. That is because animals and insects generally are better than humans at detecting odors.

When humans smell, the odor must travel to the inside of the nose before it can be processed. Animals and insects identify odors more directly. A dog, for example, has smell receptors near the tip of its nose. In addition, the dog's smell receptor sites are 100 times larger than those of humans.

outside world. It warns of dangers, such as when smelling smoke from a fire. On a subconscious level, it even contributes to being attracted to another person. The sense of smell also greatly adds to taste. For example, a blindfolded person with his or her nose plugged would have a hard time tasting the difference between a slice of raw potato and a slice of apple. The smell of these foods, however, should allow for easy identification.

FROM NOSE TO BRAIN

Smelling occurs above the nasal conchae in a region just under the brain known as the olfactory area. This area is packed with millions of small cells. Like taste buds, each olfactory cell possesses a hair-like projection. In this case, the projections are called cilia. Mucus surrounds the cilia to help trap odors and to keep the hairy objects moist. Moisture is essential because gaseous substances and wetness heighten smell. Gasoline, for example, gives off almost chokingly strong fumes, while a teaspoon of dry salt is nearly odorless.

It is thought that individual elements of odors dissolve in the mucus and then stick on the cilia. The cilia then send electrical signals to the brain through a segmented piece of bone called the ethmoidal. The brain processes the various signals and identifies what is being smelled.

Because the olfactory area is close to the region of the brain associated with emotions, mood, and memory, smells can affect feelings. Smelling a favorite food makes the mouth water and

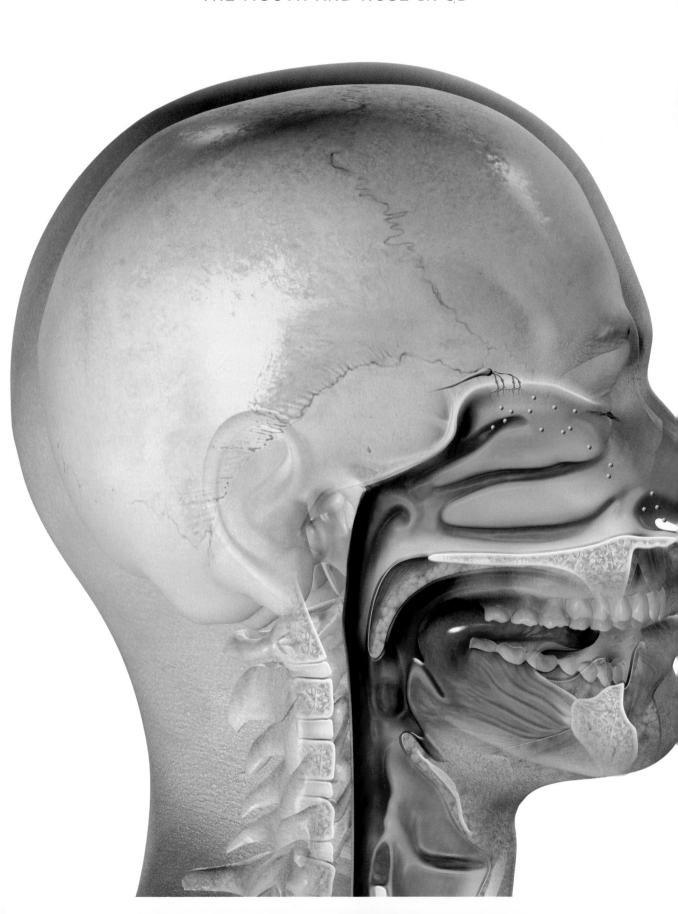

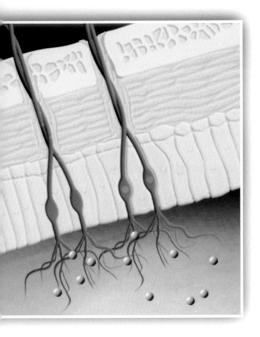

In the upper nasal cavity, or olfactory area, cilia send signals through nerve endings that lead through the eth- moidal bone and on to the brain, which detects what you smell.

creates a mental picture of what that food tastes like even before it goes into the mouth. The older people get, the more smell memories they collect. One day, the odors in place where you read this resource might trigger memories of reading up on the senses of smell and taste and all you have learned about the mouth and nose.

GLOSSARY

CARBON DIOXIDE A waste product of breathing. It is exhaled through the lungs and out of the nose.

CILIA Small, hair-like structures, such as those within the nose and throat.

DIGESTION The process of breaking down food into smaller components that can be absorbed into the bloodstream.

EPIGLOTTIS A lid-like piece of cartilage that closes off the windpipe when anything is swallowed.

ESOPHAGUS A passageway that enables food to travel from the mouth to the stomach.

GLAND An organ that produces a substance required by the body. For example, salivary glands make saliva.

LARYNX A triangular box that opens behind the tongue in the throat. It contains the vocal cords.

MANDIBLE The hinged lower part of the jaw that moves up and down to control chewing.

MAXILLA The upper part of the jaw.

MUCUS MEMBRANE A thin sheet of tissue covered with mucus, a protective slimy substance.

NASAL FOSSAE The two narrow channels in the front part of the nose.

PALATE The roof of the mouth that consists of both hard and soft parts. It separates the mouth from the nose.

PERISTALSIS Muscle contractions that send food from the throat to the stomach.

PHARYNX A muscular passage extending from the nose to the esophagus that allows for the movement of air, food, and liquids.

SALIVA A liquid containing water, mucus, an enzyme called ptyalin (which helps to break down food), and a chemical called lysozyme that has antiseptic, or germ-killing, properties.

SEPTUM The divider, made of bone and cartilage, that separates the nasal fossae.

SINUSES Cavities, or holes, in the skull that help to lessen the impact of blows to the face and also, when necessary, help to produce mucus.

TASTE BUDS Structures located in the mouth, on the tongue, and in the throat that help to identify flavors.

TRACHEA Also called the windpipe, this tube allows air to travel from the throat to the lungs.

UVULA A u-shaped extension attached to the soft palate that helps to close off nasal air passages when swallowing to prevent choking.

VOCAL CORDS Two reed-like white folds of tissue in the larynx that can move, stretch, and vibrate to produce different sounds.

FOR MORE INFORMATION

Active Healthy Kids Canada

77 Bloor Street West

Suite #1205

Toronto, Ontario M5S 1M2

Canada

Website: http://www.activehealthykids.ca

This organization's website provides information on keeping children healthy, happy, and active.

American Lung Association

55 W. Wacker Drive, Suite 1150

Chicago, IL 60601

1-800-LUNG-USA

Website: http://www.lung.org/lung-disease/asthma/in-schools

The ALA's "Open Airways for School Programs" area provides excellent information about how the respiratory system works, how to maintain it, and what to do about related medical conditions, such as asthma.

BrainPOP Health

71 W 23rd St., 17th Fl.

New York, New York 10010

Website: https://www.brainpop.com/health/bodysystems

Learn about all the different body systems, with features on smell, digestion, and teeth.

Canadian Institute of Child Health (CICH)

Suite 300, 384 Bank Street

Ottawa, ON K2P 1Y4

Canada

(613) 230-8838

Website: http://www.cich.ca

The Canadian Institute of Child Health (CICH) focuses on advancing and preserving child and youth rights and welfare through observation, knowledge, and support.

KidSource Online

1066 Kelly Dr., Ste 113

San Jose, CA 95129-3221

(408) 253-0246

Website: http://www.kidsource.com/kidsource/pages/Health.html

Provides links to virtual activities, information, and websites for children.

Teens Health

Nemours Home Office

10140 Centurion Parkway North

Jacksonville, FL 32256

(904) 697-4100

Website: http://teenshealth.org/teen/

The Teens Health website provides articles, questions and answers, and quizzes to help teens be as healthy as possible.

WEBSITES

Because of the changing nature of Internet links, Rosen Publishing has developed an online list of websites related to the subject of this book. This site is updated regularly. Please use this link to access the list:

http://www.rosenlinks.com/HB3D/Mouth

FOR FURTHER READING

Bathroom Readers' Institute. *Uncle John's Smell-O-Scopic Bathroom Reader for Kids Only!* Ashland, OR: Bathroom Readers' Press, 2013.

Jango-Cohen, Judith. *Your Respiratory System*. Minneapolis, MN: Lerner Publications Co., 2013.

Gold, Susan Dudley. *Learning About the Digestive and Excretory Systems*. Berkeley Heights, NJ: Enslow Publishers, 2013.

Gomdori Co., and Hyun-dong Han. *Inside the Human Body. Vol 1. The Digestive System*. San Francisco, CA: No Starch Press, 2013.

Koontz, Robin Michal. *Sniffs and Stinks: How Animals Use Odor to Survive*. New York, NY: Marshall Cavendish Benchmark, 2012.

Lundgren, Julie K. *Eating and the Digestive System*. Vero Beach, FL: Rourke Educational Media, 2013.

Rogers, Kara. *Ear, Nose, and Throat*. New York, NY: Britannica Educational Publishing, 2011.

Wilsdon, Christina, Patricia Daniels, Jen Agresta, and Cynthia Turner. *Ultimate body-pedia: An Amazing Inside-Out Tour of the Human Body*. Washington, DC: National Geographic Society, 2014.

INDEX

ABOUT THE AUTHORS

Isobel Towne is an author and editor specializing in science and philosophy. She lives on the coast of northern Maine where she can ramble along the rocks, observing wildlife and smelling and tasting the fresh, salty air.

Jennifer Viegas is a reporter for Discovery Channel Online News and is a feature columnist for Knight Ridder newspapers. She has worked as a journalist for ABC News, PBS, and other media. Jennifer also helped to write two cookbooks for Cooking Light that excite the senses of smell and taste.

PHOTO CREDITS

Cover, p. 1 Marlinde/Shutterstock.com; cover, p. 1 (hand) © iStockphoto.com/ Nixxphotography; p. 5 shirophoto/iStock/Thinkstock; p. 8 Simone Brandt/ Getty Images; p. 9 decade3d/iStock/Thinkstock; pp. 10, 17 Sebastian Kaulitzki/ Shutterstock.com; p. 13 Bo Veisland/Science Source; pp. 15, 37, 41 SCIEPRO/ Science Photo Library/Getty Images; pp. 16, 31 snapgalleria/Shutterstock .com; pp. 20–21, 32–33, 34–35 BSIP/Universal Images Group/Getty Images; p. 23 stockshoppe/Shutterstock.com; pp. 24–25 MediaForMedical/UIG/Getty Images; p. 26 jack0m/Digital Vision Vectors/Getty Images; p. 28 sankalpmaya/ iStock/Thinkstock; p. 29 Oliver Burston/Ikon Images/Getty Images; pp. 38–39 BSIP/Science Source; p. 45 Gwen Shockey/Science Source; pp. 46–47 Omikron Omikron/Science Source/Getty Images; p. 49 Dorling Kindersley/ Getty Images; pp. 50–51 Encyclopaedia Britannica/UIG/Getty Images; pp. 54–55 Claus Lunau/Science Source; back cover (figure) © iStockphoto.com/ comotion design; cover and interior pages graphic elements © iStockphoto .com/StudioM1, wenani/Shutterstock.com, Egor Tetiushev/Shutterstock.com.

Designer: Brian Garvey; Editor: Heather Moore Niver; Photo Researcher: Karen Huang